RANDOM
ILLUSTRATED
FACTS

RANDOM ILLUSTRATED FACTS

A COLLECTION OF CURIOUS, WEIRD, AND TOTALLY NOT BORING THINGS TO KNOW

mike LOWERY

WORKMAN PUBLISHING
NEW YORK, NY

Library of Congress Cataloging-in-Publication Data is available.

ISBN 978-0-7611-8995-4

Workman books are available at special discounts when purchased in bulk for premiums and sales promotions as well as for fund-raising or educational use. Special editions or book excerpts can also be created to specification. For details, contact the Special Sales Director at the address below, or send an email to specialmarkets@workman.com.

Workman Publishing Co., Inc.
225 Varick Street
New York, NY 10014-4381
workman.com

WORKMAN is a registered trademark of Workman Publishing Co., Inc.
Printed in China
First printing October 2017
10 9 8 7 6 5 4 3 2

A BRIEF (BUT STILL SLIGHTLY RAMBLING) INTRODUCTION

BY THE AUTHOR.

HI

I'M AN **AVID** SKETCHBOOK KEEPER. I'VE **BEEN** DOING it SINCE I WAS A **KID**, AND I'VE DRAWN in ONE DAILY FOR almost **20** YEARS. IT DIDN'T COME NATURALLY AT FIRST, BUT THEN, LIKE ANYTHING **ELSE** that GETS BETTER WITH **PRACTICE**, SO DID MY DRAWING, AND I ABSOLUTELY FELL in **LOVE** WITH KEEPING A **DAILY** RECORD of MY LIFE AND GROWTH AS AN ARTIST. & OVER the YEARS MY **SKETCHBOOK** BECAME A PLACE to **JOT** DOWN IDEAS FOR PROJECTS,

A PLACE to DOODLE AND EXPERIMENT WITH DIFFERENT types of MEDIA, AND ALSO A DIARY WHERE I made NOTES AND COMICS ABOUT MY DAY. I STARTED to KEEP SMALLER SKETCHBOOKS SO THAT I COULD CARRY them WITH ME on TRIPS, BUT ALSO TO NOT-SO-EXOTIC PLACES LIKE the DMV OR the DENTIST'S OFFICE OR A COFFEE SHOP. ... A FEW YEARS BACK, I DECIDED to DRAW SOME REALLY WEIRD thing I'D READ. It WAS ABOUT HOW A CHICKEN NUGGET HAD SOLD on EBAY FOR OVER $8,000 BECAUSE it LOOKED LIKE GEORGE WASHINGTON. OR MAYBE the FIRST ONE WAS ABOUT HOW YOU'RE MORE LIKELY to GET KILLED →

BY A **VENDING** (MACHINE) than A SHARK. I DREW it OUT, AND then DECIDED to DRAW ANOTHER ... AND then I JUST KEPT GOING. AND THIS IS HOW **RANDOM ILLUSTRATED FACTS** WAS BORN. I GOT into the ROUTINE of WAKING UP EARLY, MAKING COFFEE, AND SITTING AND READING OVER STRANGE FACTS. AND then I JUST DREW. SOMETIMES in PENCIL, SOMETIMES PEN OR BRUSH. I JUST **DREW** WITH WHATEVER I HAD WITH ME. NOW, YEARS LATER, I'VE DONE HUNDREDS of THESE FACTS.

I HATE to SPOIL the SURPRISE FOR YOU, BUT AS SOON AS you TURN the PAGE, YOU'RE going to SEE them.

— miKE LOWERY

PART

ONE

RANDOM FACTS ABOUT
HISTORY:

- - - - - - - - - - - - - - - - - -

MID-FLIGHT DUELS, THE ORIGINAL BEAUTY MARK,
and AL CAPONE'S BUSINESS CARD

IN 1910 SOME PEOPLE BOUGHT ANTI COMET PILLS BECAUSE THEY WERE AFRAID of BEING GASSED BY the TAIL OF HALLEY'S COMET.

IN the 1800s, 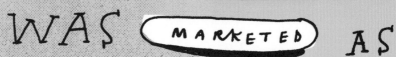 WAS MARKETED AS A REMEDY for FUSSY - - - - - - BABIES.

QUIETNESS

A SHEEP, A DUCK, and a ROOSTER WERE the FIRST PASSENGERS ON A HOT AIR BALLOON.

HOT AIR BALLOONS

1 THE TRADITION OF HAVING CHAMPAGNE AFTER A FLIGHT WAS STARTED TO APPEASE THE FARMERS WHO DIDN'T WANT BALLOONS LANDING ON THEIR PROPERTY.

APPEASED

3 EEEEEK!

A GLASS-BOTTOM BALLOON WAS INVENTED AND HAD THE PASSENGERS SCREAMING in FEAR MIDFLIGHT.

2 THIS WAS A BAD IDEA.

IN 1808, TWO MEN DUELED in HOT AIR BALLOONS. THE BALLOON THAT WAS SHOT CRASHED TO THE GROUND.

DANIEL BOONE

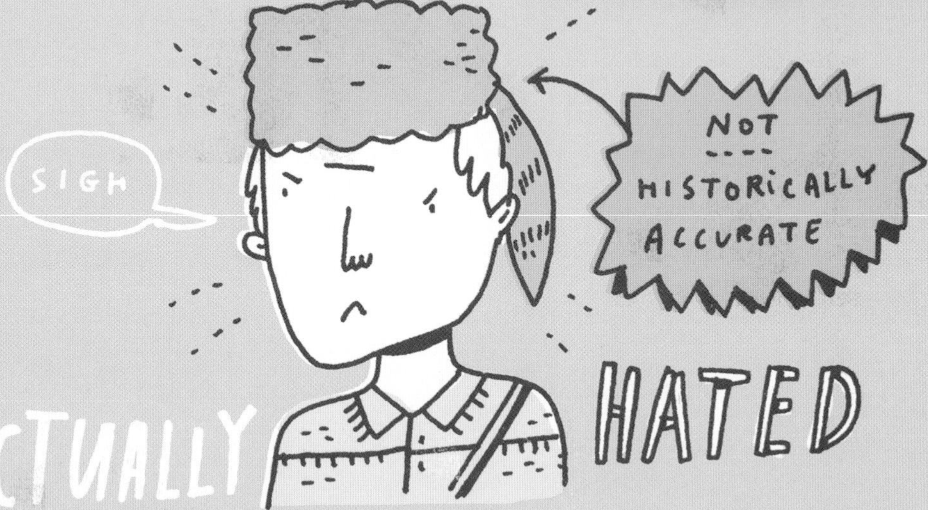

ACTUALLY HATED COONSKIN CAPS.

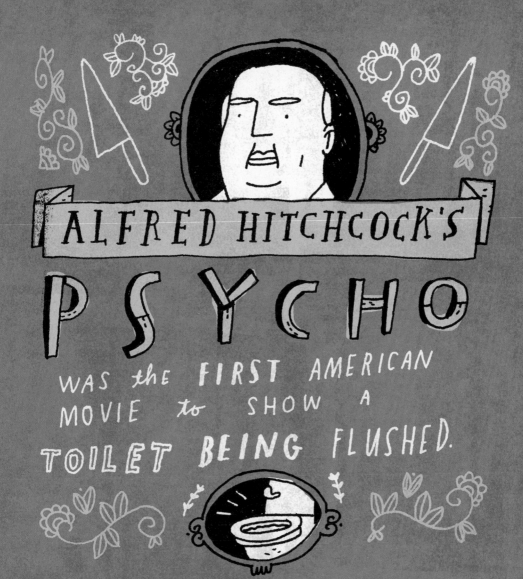

ALFRED HITCHCOCK'S

PSYCHO

WAS the FIRST AMERICAN MOVIE to SHOW A TOILET BEING FLUSHED.

SOME HISTORIANS THINK VINCENT VAN GOGH DIDN'T CUT off HIS OWN EAR, BUT THAT PAINTER PAUL GAUGUIN DID IT WITH A SWORD.

LOOK →

A FEW things ABOUT

ARTISTS

1 SALVADOR DALÍ

BELIEVED HE WAS his DEAD BROTHER REINCARNATED.

2 ANDY WARHOL WANTED TO OPEN "A RESTAURANT FOR THE LONELY PERSON" WHERE YOU COULD TAKE YOUR TRAY TO A BOOTH AND WATCH TV.

3 ONE of HENRI MATISSE'S PIECES HUNG UPSIDE DOWN for 47 DAYS BEFORE SOMEONE NOTICED.

LOOKS FINE TO ME!

EDGAR ALLAN POE

1. INVENTED MODERN DETECTIVE STORIES.

2. PUBLISHED his FIRST BOOK at 18.

3. MARRIED his FIRST COUSIN (he WAS 27, SHE WAS 13).

4. WAS BURIED in an UNMARKED GRAVE in BALTIMORE. 26 YEARS LATER TEACHERS, STUDENTS, and PUBLISHERS raised MONEY FOR a MONUMENT.

FAMOUS QUOTES

THAT WERE NEVER ACTUALLY SAID

"LET them EAT CAKE." — MARIE ANTOINETTE

"YOU DIRTY RAT." — JAMES CAGNEY

"PLAY IT AGAIN, SAM." — RICK BLAINE

"ELEMENTARY, MY DEAR WATSON." — SHERLOCK HOLMES

"BEAM ME UP, SCOTTY." — CAPTAIN KIRK

the WRIGHT BROS'

① THEY DECIDED WHO WOULD **FLY FIRST** WITH A **COIN TOSS**.

② THEY OWNED A **BICYCLE** REPAIR SHOP.

③ THEY PROMISED THEIR DAD THEY WOULD (NEVER) FLY TOGETHER in CASE there WAS AN **ACCIDENT**.

④ **NEIL** ARMSTRONG CARRIED A PIECE of THEIR PLANE TO THE **MOON**.

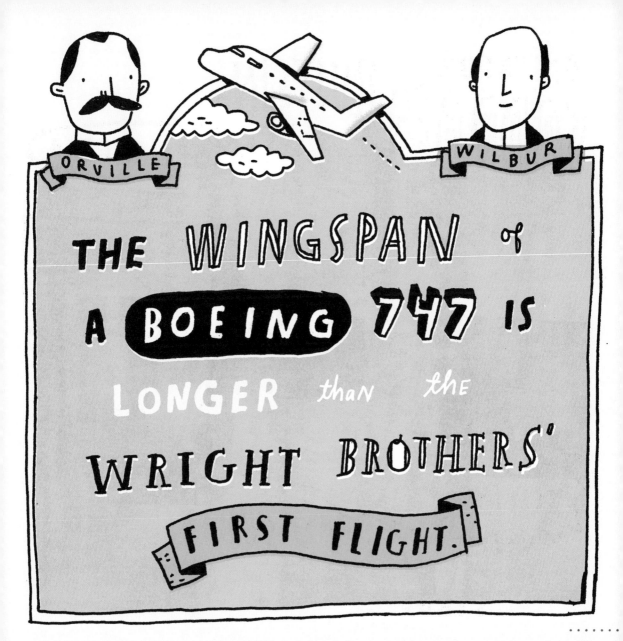

ORVILLE

WILBUR

THE WINGSPAN of A **BOEING** 747 IS LONGER than the WRIGHT BROTHERS' FIRST FLIGHT.

Dictator SADDAM HUSSEIN ANONYMOUSLY PUBLISHED A ROMANCE NOVEL THAT WAS LATER MADE into a BEST-SELLING TV SERIES and STAGE MUSICAL.

A FEW FACTS ABOUT the OLYMPICS

THE ANCIENT OLYMPIANS COMPETED COMPLETELY NAKED.

FROM 1984 TO 1992 SOLO SYNCHRONIZED SWIMMING WAS AN OLYMPIC SPORT.

FROM 1912 TO 1948 ARTISTS ALSO COMPETED IN the OLYMPIC GAMES.

BLUSH

I DO SHOT PUT, YOU?

WHO, ME?

BEN FRANKLIN

WROTE A SERIES OF 14 LETTERS MAKING FUN of EVERYTHING FROM FUNERAL EULOGIES TO THE STUDENTS at HARVARD. HE ASSUMED THE PERSONA of A MIDDLE-AGED WOMAN and SIGNED THEM WITH THE PSEUDONYM SILENCE DOGOOD.

BEN FRANKLIN

ALSO DESIGNED ONE of THE FIRST

U. S. — FUGIO — 1787 — COINS.

INSTEAD of "IN GOD WE TRUST,"
IT SAID "**MIND**
YOUR BUSINESS."

AL CAPONE'S BUSINESS CARD

CAPONE'S FURNITURE

WE'LL MURDER the COMPETITION.

SAID that HE WAS A USED FURNITURE SALESMAN.

THE RACING HALL of FAME HONORS MORE HORSES than JOCKEYS.

ANCIENT ROMANS SAW A UNIBROW AS A SYMBOL of **BEAUTY.** **ANCIENT GREEKS** WORE FALSE BROWS MADE OUT **OF GOAT HAIR.**

IN the **MIDDLE AGES** the FOREHEAD WAS CONSIDERED SO ATTRACTIVE, WOMEN WOULD REMOVE their **EYE BROWS** to ACCENTUATE IT.

IN PRE-REVOLUTION FRANCE, PALE SKIN WAS IDOLIZED and WOMEN WOULD DRAW VEINS on their <u>NECKS AND SHOULDERS.</u>

COMPOSED HIS FIRST SYMPHONY
AT THE AGE OF 8.

THE WORD PRODIGY COMES FROM
THE LATIN FOR

"OMEN" OR "MONSTER."

IN 2011, THE ENTIRE COUNTRY OF LIECHTENSTEIN COULD BE RENTED FOR $70,000 A NIGHT.

LIECHTENSTEIN.

① WORLD'S LEADER in PRODUCTION of

FALSE  TEETH.

③ SWITZERLAND ACCIDENTALLY INVADED IT ONCE.

② IN 1866 DURING ITS LAST BATTLE FOR INDEPENDENCE,

80 SOLDIERS LEFT AND 81 RETURNED.

(THEY PICKED UP A NEW AUSTRIAN FRIEND.)

OOPS!

LIECHTENSTEIN

37

POLAR BEARS DON'T NEED SUNGLASSES.

BUT I DO LOOK AMAZING in THEM.

THEY HAVE A 3RD EYELID that HELPS them FILTER OUT UV LIGHT.

THE 1ST SUNGLASSES in CHINA WERE WORN BY JUDGES to HIDE THEIR EMOTIONS.

IN THE EARLY 20TH CENTURY, SOME PEOPLE WORE ELECTRIC GLASSES, WHICH CLAIMED TO IMPROVE EYESIGHT (THEY DIDN'T).

THE FIRST VISION-CORRECTING DEVICE WAS A GLASS MOUND CALLED A READING STONE.

I GOT THE WRONG THING

JUST A ROCK

39

PART

TWO

RANDOM FACTS ABOUT

ANIMALS:

EXPLOSIVE ANTS, LIFE-LOVING LEMMINGS, and ONE REALLY **FAT** REINDEER

FROGS!

1 MANY FROGS shed all of (THEIR SKIN) ONCE A WEEK.

2 A SINGLE GOLDEN POISON DART FROG HOLDS ENOUGH POISON TO KILL **10** PEOPLE.

3 A GROUP of FROGS is CALLED AN ARMY.

4 SOME GLASS FROGS HAVE SEE-THROUGH SKIN SO YOU CAN SEE THEIR INTERNAL ORGANS, **BONES**, and MUSCLES.

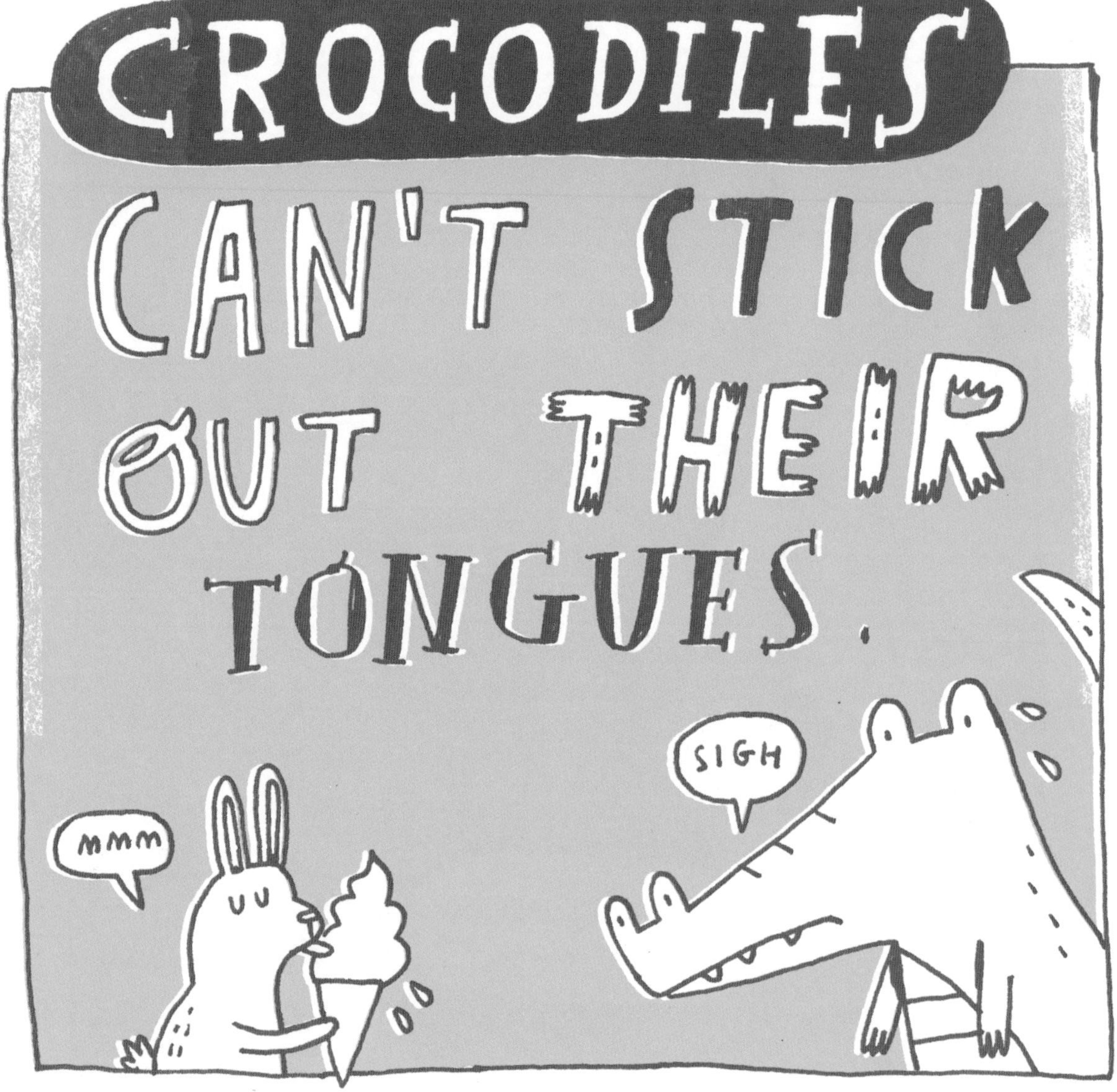
CROCODILES
CAN'T STICK
OUT THEIR
TONGUES.
MMM
SIGH

IN (2007) A BOWHEAD WHALE WAS FOUND WITH PART of A HARPOON FROM THE 1880S in ITS NECK.

HOUSEFLIES

always **BUZZ** in the key of **F**

which is good because I only know three chords.

FLIES:

1. "USE their ANTENNAE to SMELL.

2. LAY EGGS that HATCH IN A MATTER of HOURS.

3. *mmmm* SUCK UP their FOOD WITH A LONG TONGUE-LIKE ORGAN CALLED A PROBOSCIS.

4. HAVE EYES THAT CAN TRACK MOVEMENT 5 TIMES FASTER THAN HUMANS!

5. CAN FLAP THEIR WINGS 200 TIMES PER SECOND.

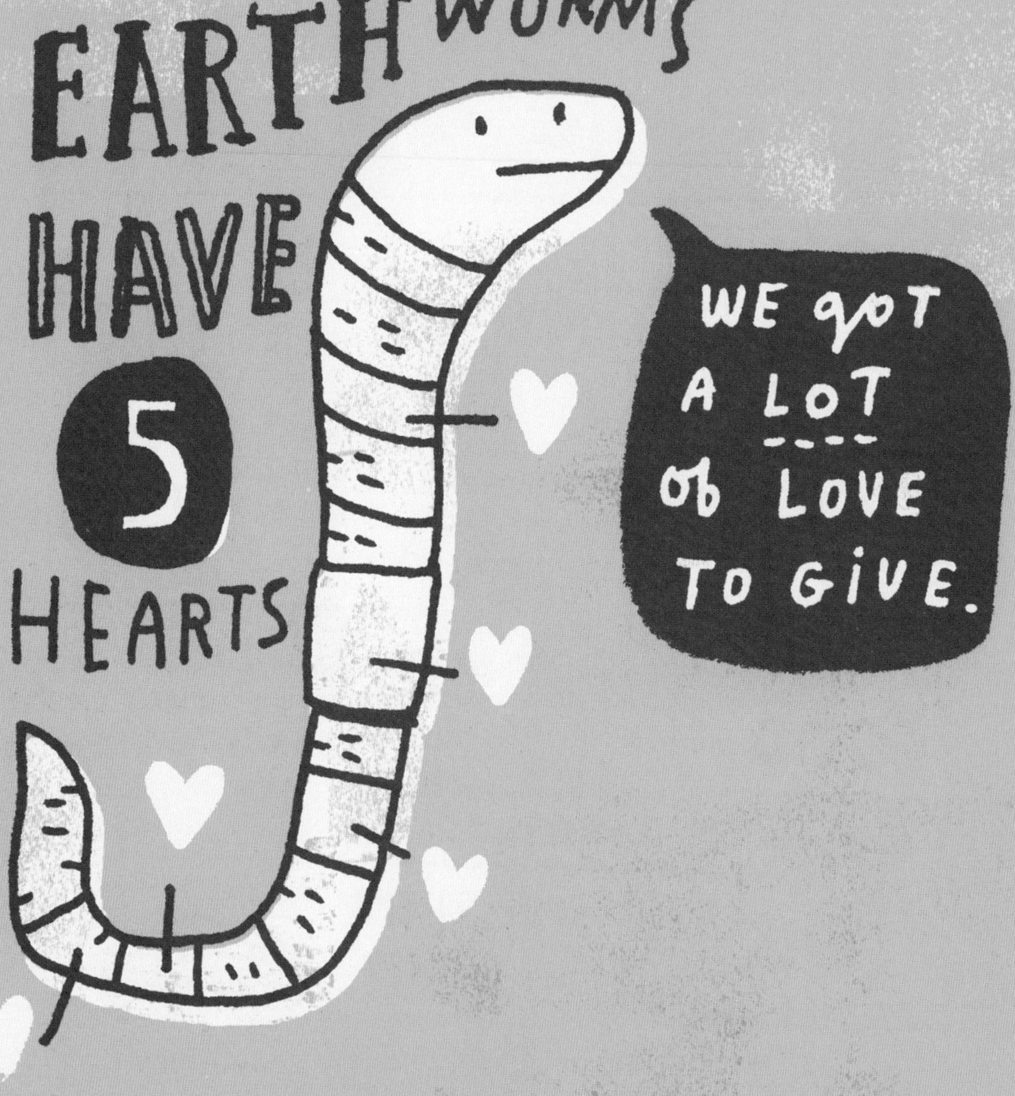
EARTHWORMS HAVE 5 HEARTS
WE got A LOT of LOVE TO GIVE.

A cat in RUSSIA kept an ABANDONED NEWBORN BABY ALIVE in BELOW-FREEZing temperatures.

LET'S TALK ABOUT POISON

THERE WAS A LOCAL LEGEND of AN EVIL SPIRIT WHO DESTROYED PARTS of THE AMAZON RAIN FOREST. IT WAS LATER DISCOVERED TO BE POISONOUS ANTS.

VMM

HAIRBALLS PEOPLE THOUGHT WERE ANTIDOTES TO POISON and WOULD EAT THEM!

THE GRASSHOPPER MOUSE, WHICH EATS SCORPIONS, IS IMMUNE TO THEIR POISON.

GIRAFFES ONLY NEED 4.6 HOURS OF SLEEP A DAY.

I NEED A LITTLE MORE.

ZZZZZZZ

1 IN 30 PEOPLE SLEEP-WALK.

A BEDBUG CAN GO 2 TO 3 MONTHS WITHOUT FEEDING.

WHY WOULD YOU TELL ME THAT?!

THE WORD "NIGHTMARE" ORIGINALLY DESCRIBED AN EVIL SPIRIT THAT SUFFOCATED YOU WHILE YOU SLEPT.

65% of THE WATER in A WOOD FROG'S BODY TURNS into ICE DURING THEIR HIBERNATION.

GROUNDHOG

ZZZZZ

FACTS

They are one of the few animals that truly HIBERNATE, a dormant state where their heart rate drops to 5 BEATS PER MINUTE!

ALSO KNOWN AS WOODCHUCKS or WHISTLE-PIGS.

THEIR INCISORS GROW 1/16 of an inch EACH WEEK.

THEIR BURROWS CAN GO ON FOR 20 FEET UNDERGROUND AND CAN HAVE UP TO A DOZEN ENTRANCES.

LET'S LEARN ABOUT

COCKROACHES

1 THEY CAN HOLD their **BREATH** for up to **40** min. (SO FLUSHING THEM DOWN the TOILET WON'T ALWAYS **KILL** THEM.)

2 SOME COCKROACHES ARE MONOGAMOUS.

NOT THIS ONE

HEY GIRL

BRR

3 SOME will HIBERNATE BY **FREEZING** in the **SNOW** and THAWING WHEN THE TEMPERATURE **WARMS** up.

4 IN SOME COUNTRIES THEY ARE A DELICACY AND ARE SERVED **DEEP-FRIED.**

A COCKROACH CAN LIVE FOR WEEKS WITHOUT ITS HEAD

GRUMBLE GRUMBLE

BEFORE IT STARVES TO DEATH.

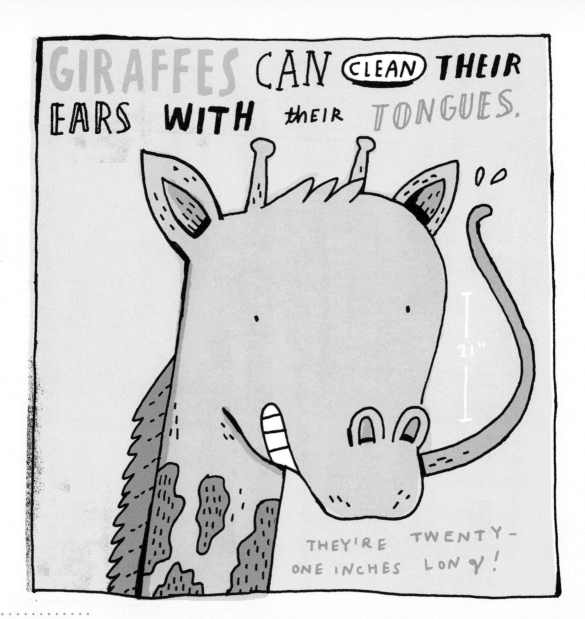

TONGUE

STICKING FACTS

OUT your TONGUE IS A Greeting in **TIBET**.

THE AVERAGE PERSON HAS BETWEEN 2,000 AND

10,000 TASTE BUDS

AND THEY'RE REPLACED EVERY ONE TO TWO WEEKS.

A CHAMELEON'S TONGUE CAN GO FROM 0 TO 60 mPH in 1/100TH OF A SECOND.

A BLUE WHALE'S TONGUE WEIGHS ABOUT 3 TONS.

BATS!

POLLEN

AGAVE PLANT

WITHOUT BATS WE WOULDN'T HAVE **TEQUILA**.

GUANO (BAT DROPPINGS) IS USED AS FERTILIZER in SOME **TROPICAL REGIONS**.

SOME BATS CAN EAT up to **1,200** MOSQUITOES IN AN HOUR.

HI

THE BUMBLEBEE BAT is the WORLD'S smallest **BAT**. THEY ARE SMALLER THAN YOUR PALM and LIGHTER THAN A PENNY.

BATS ARE the ONLY MAMMALS that **CAN FLY**.

A LARGE GROUP of BATS IN THE SKY IS CALLED A "CLOUD."

BEES in FRANCE, FOUND to PRODUCE **BLUE** and GREEN HONEY, TURNED OUT to BE EATING WASTE FROM A LOCAL CANDY FACTORY

YUM.

BZZZZ

SOME STUFF ABOUT DUCKS

A GROUP of DUCKS is called A RAFT.

A DUCK HAS A HARD NAIL ON the END of ITS BILL.

THEIR QUACKS <u>DO</u> ECHO.

A MALE DUCK:
DRAKE

A FEMALE DUCK:
HEN

A CAT in TALKEETNA, ALASKA,

mayor STUBBS

HAS BEEN MAYOR

for →

YEARS.

A FEW RANDOM CAT FACTS

① THE *technical* NAME FOR A HAIRBALL IS A BEZOAR. SORRY

② A GROUP of CATS IS called A CLOWDER.

③ DURING *the* MIDDLE AGES CATS WERE ASSOCIATED WITH WITCHCRAFT. WHO ME?

DURING WW II, POLISH SOLDIERS ADOPTED A BEAR.

CZEŚĆ

HE WRESTLED WITH SOLDIERS, CARRIED AMMUNITION, and DRANK BEER.

BEARS

① TO STORE UP **FAT**, A GRIZZLY BEAR WILL EAT **90** POUNDS OF FOOD PER DAY LEADING UP TO ITS **HIBERNATION**.

② **IF YOU ATE A** POLAR **BEAR'S** LIVER, YOU COULD DIE OF A **VITAMIN A OVERDOSE**.

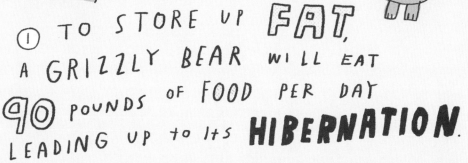

③ A PREGNANT BEAR WILL WAKE UP FROM HIBERNATION TO GIVE BIRTH AND WILL CONTINUE TO NURSE HER CUBS EVEN AFTER SHE'S RETURNED TO HIBERNATING.

SOME **YOGA** STUDIOS OFFER CLASSES

WITH **GOATS.**

WHALES DON'T BLOW WATER OUT OF THEIR BLOWHOLES.

(IT'S JUST THEIR HOT BREATH CONDENSING AS IT REACHES THE COOL OUTSIDE AIR, GIVING THE APPEARANCE OF WATER!)

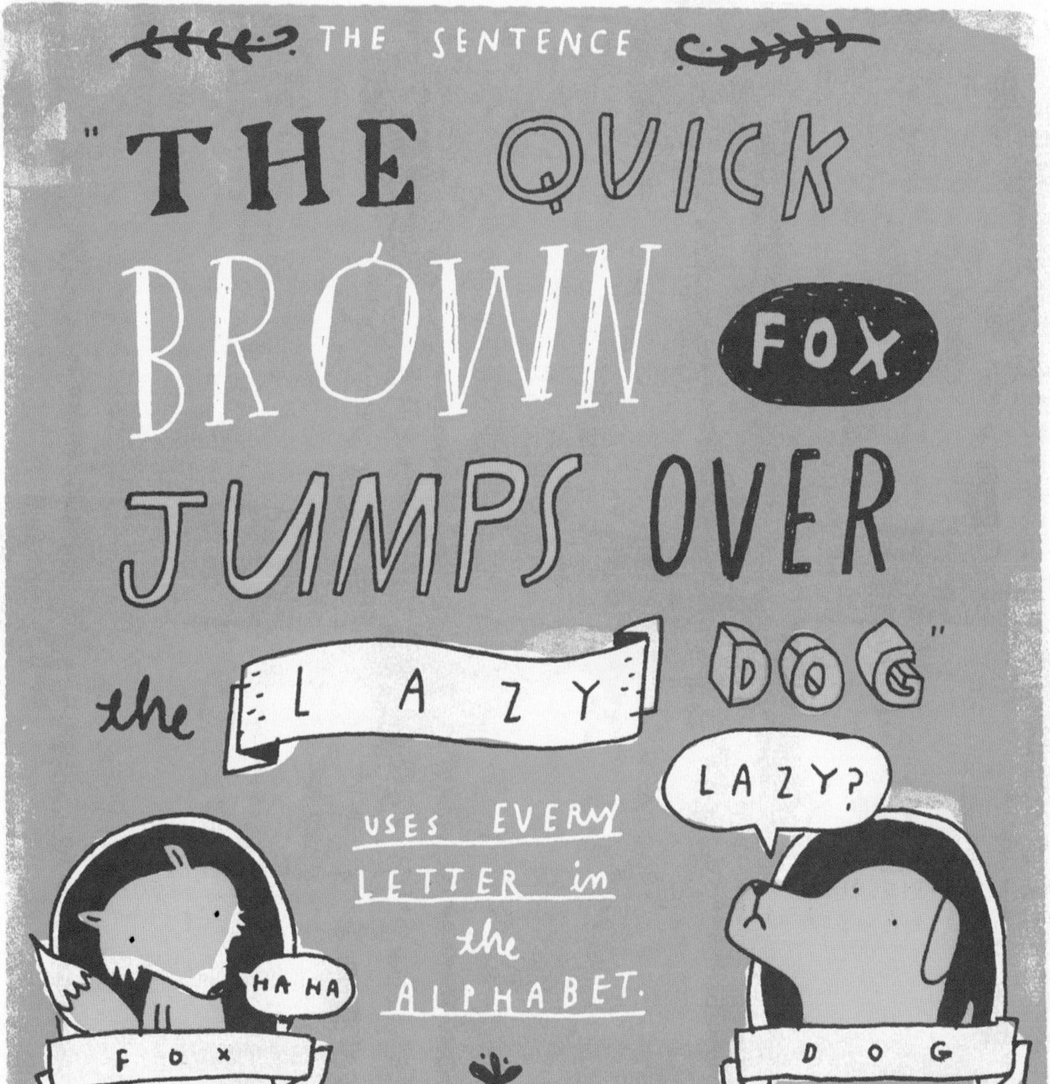

"THE QUICK BROWN FOX JUMPS OVER the LAZY DOG"

LAZY?

USES EVERY LETTER in the ALPHABET.

HA HA

FOX

DOG

MORE
FACTS ABOUT HAIR

① BLACK is the MOST COMMON hair COLOR in the WORLD. RED IS the RAREST.

② THE ONLY PARTS OF THE BODY THAT CAN'T GROW HAIR ARE THE PALMS, THE SOLES OF YOUR FEET, AND YOUR LIPS.

③ DURING the VICTORIAN AGE, PEOPLE WOULD WEAR JEWELRY MADE FROM the HAIR of DEAD PEOPLE (LOST LOVED ONES).

A TERMITE QUEEN CAN LIVE UP TO 25 YEARS.

"??"

I'M OLD ENOUGH TO RENT A CAR,

BUT THEY STILL WON'T LET ME.

MAYFLIES HAVE the
SHORTEST ADULT LIFE AMONG
INSECTS: THEY ONLY HAVE
5 MINUTES AFTER EMERGING
FROM thEIR NYMPH PHASE
TO MATE AND LAY EGGS
BEFORE DYING!

PART

THREE

HELLO!

RANDOM FACTS ABOUT

FOOD AND DRINKS:

DELICIOUS DISCOVERIES, GROSS BUT
REAL SNACKS, and ROBOTS that
LICK LOLLIPOPS

COFFEE

IN JAPAN there ARE CAT CAFÉS where you can HANG OUT with CATS.

MOSHI MOSHI

猫 =

TEDDY ROOSEVELT WAS RUMORED to DRINK ONE GALLON of COFFEE A DAY!

DUNKIN' DONUTS ONCE USED A FAKE COFFEE SCENT ON BUSES to LURE COMMUTERS IN SOUTH KOREA.

THE SAUCER HAS BEEN USED BY SOME AS A PLACE TO POUR COFFEE TO COOL IT BEFORE SIPPING.

LEGEND HAS IT that COFFEE WAS DISCOVERED WHEN ETHIOPIAN SHEPHERDS SAW THEIR GOATS "DANCING" AFTER EATING COFFEE BERRIES.

TA DA!

THERE IS A CHEESE in SARDINIA that CONTAINS LIVE MAGGOTS.

FOOD TIDBITS

A FEW FACTS TO CHEW ON

① IN the 1830s A KETCHUP WAS SOLD AS A REMEDY FOR DIARRHEA.

It's NOT HELPING.

EW

② ARACHIBUTYROPHOBIA IS the FEAR of PEANUT BUTTER sticking TO the ROOF OF your MOUTH.

③ THE SHINY COATING ON JELLY BEANS IS MADE FROM STICKY GOO SECRETED BY BUGS.

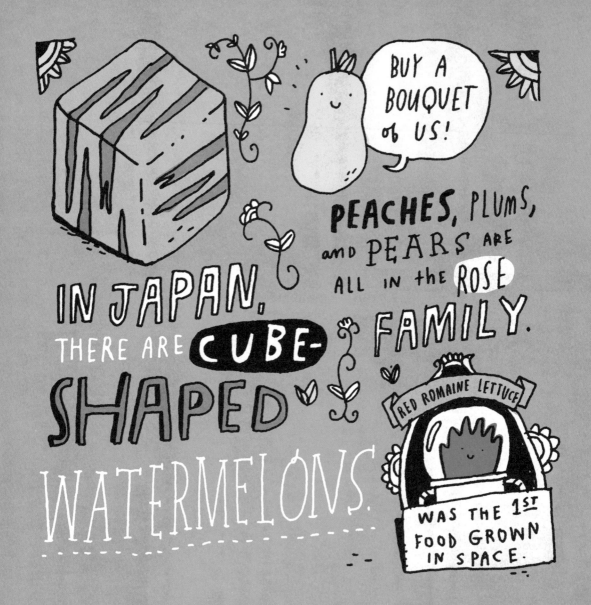

RAMEN FACTS

270 MILLION SERVINGS of INSTANT RAMEN ARE EATEN EVERY DAY.

INSTANT RAMEN NOODLES WERE FIRST TAKEN INTO SPACE IN 2005.

CHINA EATS MORE RAMEN than ANY OTHER COUNTRY.

IN JAPAN THERE ARE VENDING MACHINES THAT SERVE HOT INSTANT RAMEN.

LEMONS

1. MEDIEVAL EGYPTIANS CREATED LEMONADE BUT THEY CALLED IT QATARZIMAT.

2. THE WORLD'S HEAVIEST LEMON WAS ALMOST 12 LBS.

Hi

3. CHRISTOPHER COLUMBUS INTRODUCED LEMONS to the AMERICAS in 1493.

"WHEN LIFE GIVES YOU LEMONS, MAKE **LEMONADE**"

WAS MADE FAMOUS BECAUSE IT WAS USED IN AN ACTOR'S OBITUARY.

THE "ADE" AT THE END MEANS IT'S NOT 100% JUICE.

THE AVERAGE **LEMON** HAS ROUGHLY 3 TABLESPOONS OF JUICE.

LEMONS ARE TECHNICALLY BERRIES.

NATIVE ALASKANS HAVE A UNIQUE type of ICE CREAM THAT CONTAINS INGREDIENTS LIKE REINDEER FAT, SEAL OIL, FRESH SNOW, and BERRIES.

ICE CREAM

Yummy Yummy

1. THERE'S A TREE in SOUTH AMERICA THAT GROWS BEANS *that* TASTE LIKE **VANILLA ICE CREAM.**

2. SMURF *the* COW

OOF

HOLDS THE RECORD FOR MOST **MILK** PRODUCED in A LIFETIME: **478,163** LBS!

3. SOME **ICE CREAM** TESTERS USE A GOLDEN SPOON *to* **AVOID** *the* AFTERTASTE FROM REGULAR SPOONS.

GUM

1. THE LARGEST BUBBLE EVER BLOWN WAS 20 INCHES IN DIAMETER.

2. IN 2007 AN ARCHAEOLOGY STUDENT FOUND A 5,000-YEAR-OLD PIECE OF GUM.

3. THE FIRST COMMERCIAL BUBBLE GUM WAS CALLED BLIBBER-BLUBBER.

A STUDENT FROM THE UNIVERSITY OF MICHIGAN RECORDED THAT HIS CUSTOMIZED LICKING MACHINE REQUIRED 411 LICKS TO REACH the CENTER of A TOOTSIE POP.

PIZZA

ICE CREAM

WEIRD,

FOOD FACTS

BUT

TRUE

HAGGIS

HORSE MEAT

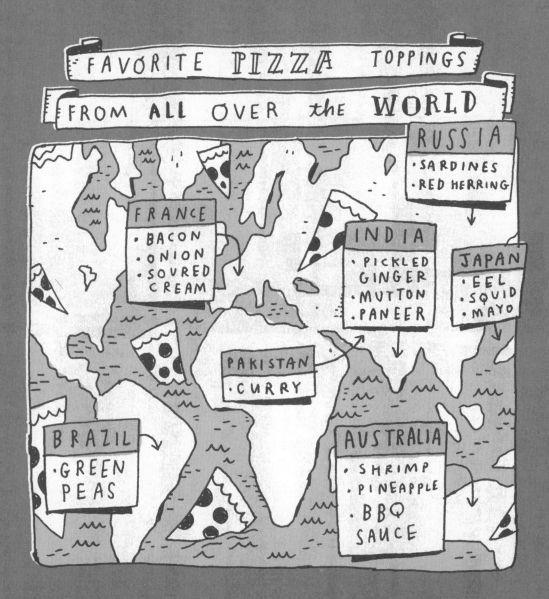

STRANGE ICE CREAM FLAVORS
(THAT ACTUALLY EXIST)

RAW HORSE MEAT
(JAPAN)

HAGGIS
(SCOTLAND)

BREAST MILK
(ENGLAND)

SMOKED SALMON
(USA)

OCTOPUS
(JAPAN)

GARLIC
(VARIOUS)

ROUGHEYE ROCKFISH CAN LIVE UP TO 205 YEARS!

PROST!
CHEERS!

SKÅL!
CHOK DEE!

LET'S HEAR it for

BEER!

1 A WAVE of BEER FLOODED LONDON in 1814 (UP TO 388,000 gallons).

2 BEER WASN'T CONSIDERED ALCOHOL in RUSSIA UNTIL 2013.

3 THE WORKERS WHO BUILT the EGYPTIAN PYRAMIDS RECEIVED about 4 LITERS of BEER A DAY.

4 BEER COMMERCIALS in the U.S. AREN'T ALLOWED TO SHOW PEOPLE DRINKING ----> BEER.

IN the 1500s, WHEN CHILI PEPPERS WERE INTRODUCED IN JAPAN, PEOPLE DIDN'T EAT them -- they put THEM in their SHOES to WARM their FEET.

hello!

スパイシー

ACCORDING TO the UNITED STATES POSTAL SERVICE,

STAMPS

HAVE ZERO CALORIES.

EATING CELERY BURNS MORE CALORIES THAN IT CONTAINS.

IT CAN TAKE A SLOTH UP to 30 DAYS TO DIGEST ONE LEAF.

TO SET A RECORD, A WOMAN ONCE ate A 30,000-CALORIE CHRISTMAS DINNER in 2 hours.

TWO 25-LB TURKEYS

TWO MAPLE-GLAZED HAMS

15 LBS OF POTATOES

5 LOAVES OF BREAD

5 LBS OF STUFFING

4 PINTS OF CRANBERRY DRESSING

4 PINTS OF GRAVY

OVER 15 LBS OF VEGGIES! →

UNPOPPED

POPCORN KERNELS ARE KNOWN AS "OLD MAIDS" OR "SPINSTERS" (WHEN FOUND at the BOTTOM of THE BOWL).

IN 2011, CHEESE WAS STOLEN MORE than ANY OTHER FOOD.

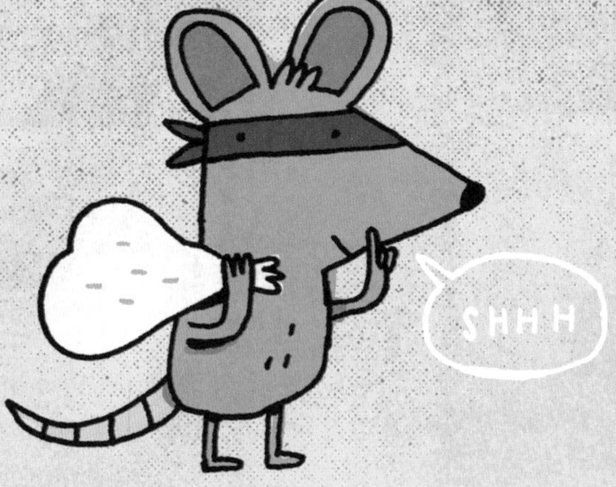

IN ANCIENT ROME, PEOPLE WOULD PUT A PIECE OF BURNT BREAD IN WINE TO SOAK UP THE ACIDITY. THIS BECAME LINKED WITH THE RITUAL OF DRINKING TO ONE'S HEALTH, OR TOASTING.

UMM

Yuck.

BREAD BITS

① THE LARGEST LOAF OF BREAD EVER BAKED WAS ALMOST **3,500 LBS.**

Hi.

② IN 1943 THE U.S. GOVERNMENT BRIEFLY ISSUED A BAN ON SLICED BREAD.

③ SANDWICHES ARE NAMED AFTER AN ENGLISH NOBLEMAN, THE EARL OF SANDWICH, WHO DEMANDED AN EASY MEAL HE COULD EAT WITHOUT GETTING UP.

④ SOME ANCIENT CULTURES WOULD USE MOLDY BREAD TO TREAT WOUNDS.

A FEW LITTLE GARDEN FACTS

THE FRENCH CALL the TOMATO the "APPLE of LOVE".

MANY BELIEVE that CONTAMINATED CHERRIES KILLED PRESIDENT ZACHARY TAYLOR.

WHAT?!

AN AVERAGE STRAWBERRY HAS ABOUT 200 SEEDS.

YUM

A HORNWORM CAN KILL an ENTIRE TOMATO PLANT in ONE DAY.

BLACK, GREEN, WHITE, AND OOLONG TEA ALL COME FROM THE SAME PLANT.

YAY!

CAKE!

ONE TRADITION SAYS THAT IF YOU PUT A SLICE of WEDDING CAKE UNDER YOUR PILLOW, YOU'LL DREAM OF YOUR FUTURE SPOUSE.

THE TALLEST CAKE EVER WAS MORE THAN 108 FEET TALL.

SONYA THOMAS ATE ALMOST 5 POUNDS OF FRUIT CAKE in TEN MINUTES TO SET A NEW RECORD.

INTERESTING!

PART

FOUR

RANDOM FACTS ABOUT
SCIENCE:

YOUR WEIRD BODY, NATURE'S WONDERS, AND OUTER SPACE

WHILE in SPACE, ASTRONAUTS CAN GROW UP TO 2" taller.

IF YOU FELL INTO A BLACK HOLE, IT'S BELIEVED YOU WOULD STRETCH INTO A LONG, THIN SHAPE → LIKE A NOODLE.

DUE TO ITS LACK of WIND, THE FOOTPRINTS LEFT ON THE MOON IN 1969 ARE PERFECTLY PRESERVED.

129

ASTRONOMER

CARL SAGAN

CREATED A GOLD-PLATED COPPER RECORD that WAS SENT into SPACE. ON IT IS A MESSAGE to ANY INTELLIGENT LIFE THAT MAY FIND IT.

SOUNDS INCLUDE
• SPOKEN GREETINGS in 55 LANGUAGES
• CLASSICAL MUSIC • "JOHNNY B. GOODE"
• THUNDER • A KISS • AND MANY MORE!

STARS

THERE ARE MORE STARS in THE UNIVERSE THAN...

- ALL the GRAINS OF SAND ON ALL THE WORLD'S BEACHES.
- ALL the WORDS AND SOUNDS EVER UTTERED BY ALL THE HUMANS WHO HAVE EVER LIVED.
- ALL the SECONDS that HAVE PASSED SINCE the EARTH FORMED.

SINCE STAR EXPLOSIONS CREATED ALL THE BASIC INGREDIENTS OF LIFE, WE ARE LITERALLY MADE OF STARDUST.

STARS DON'T ACTUALLY TWINKLE. THEY JUST APPEAR TO TWINKLE BECAUSE OF TURBULENCE.

A CHURCH STEEPLE in GERMANY WAS DESTROYED BY LIGHTNING and REBUILT ④ TIMES BETWEEN 1599 and 1783. EACH TIME it WAS STRUCK, the DATE WAS APRIL 18.

SACHEN GIBT'S, DIE GIBT'S GAR NICHT.

TEETH FACTS

A NARWHAL'S TUSK IS ACTUALLY A TOOTH that HAS GROWN THROUGH ITS UPPER LIP.

GEORGE WASHINGTON HAD FALSE TEETH MADE OUT OF IVORY, GOLD, AND LEAD, BUT NOT WOOD.

ASTRONAUT BUZZ ALDRIN'S toothBRUSH WAS AUCTIONED off FOR $22,705.

AN OLD GERMAN FOLK REMEDY FOR A TOOTHACHE WAS to KISS A DONKEY.

HAIR

HUMAN HAIR IS USED TO **CLEAN** UP **OIL** SPILLS.

THE LONGEST **BEARD** **EVER** WAS 17 FEET 6 INCHES LONG.

A SINGLE HAIR HAS A LIFE SPAN OF 2 TO 7 YEARS.

RIP

THE SCIENTIFIC term FOR SPLIT ENDS IS TRICHOPTILOSIS.

RED HAIR ONLY EXISTS in 1-2% of the WORLD POPULATION.

IT'S JUST A MYTH THAT YOUR HAIR WILL KEEP GROWING AFTER you DIE.

OOH LA LA!

YOUR SKIN JUST DRIES UP AND RECEDES MAKING IT LOOK LIKE YOUR HAIR AND NAILS ARE LONGER.

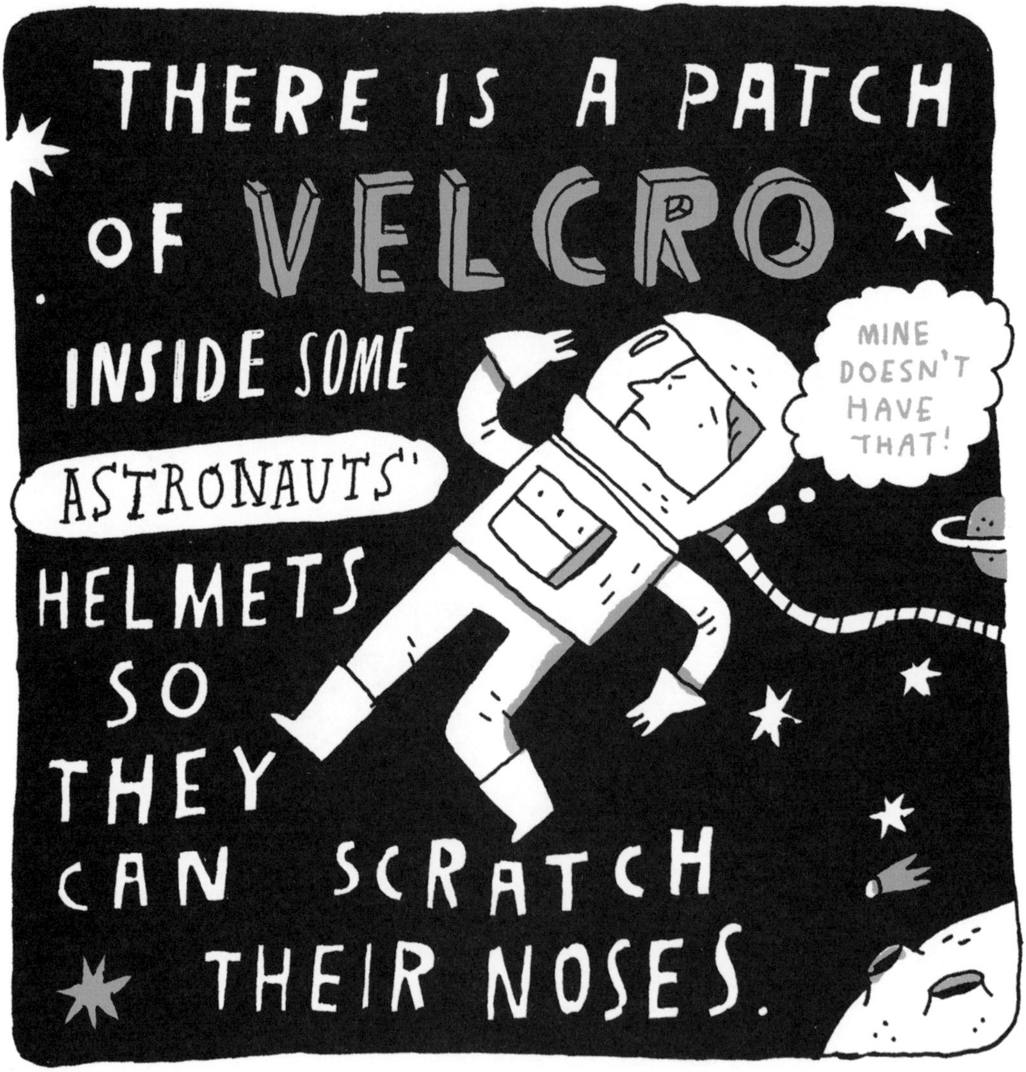
THERE IS A PATCH OF VELCRO INSIDE SOME ASTRONAUTS' HELMETS SO THEY CAN SCRATCH THEIR NOSES.
MINE DOESN'T HAVE THAT!

PUTTING ON A **SPACE SUIT** IS CALLED **DONNING.** TAKING ONE OFF IS CALLED **DOFFING.**

HALLEY'S COMET

PASSED BY THE YEAR **MARK TWAIN** WAS BORN and **AGAIN** THE YEAR HE **DIED.**

I DIDN'T SEE IT EITHER TIME.

IN SPACE, ASTRONAUTS CAN'T FEEL if THEIR BLADDER is **FULL**, SO THEY ARE TRAINED to GO EVERY **FEW** HOURS.

THE WORD (ASTRONAUT) COMES FROM the GREEK WORDS "ASTRON NAUTES", WHICH TRANSLATES TO STAR SAILOR.

ASTRONAUTS USE LIQUID SALT and PEPPER.

THE DARK SIDE OF THE MOON IS A MYTH! BOTH FACES GET SUNLIGHT BUT WE CAN ONLY SEE ONE SIDE FROM EARTH.

EARTH IS THE ONLY PLANET NOT NAMED AFTER A GOD.

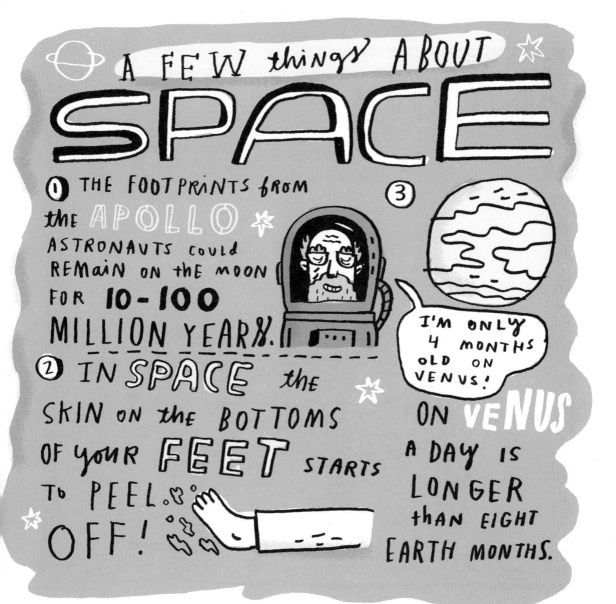

A FEW things ABOUT

SPACE

① THE FOOTPRINTS from the APOLLO ASTRONAUTS could REMAIN ON THE MOON FOR **10-100** MILLION YEARS.

② IN SPACE the SKIN ON the BOTTOMS OF your FEET STARTS To PEEL OFF!

③

I'M ONLY 4 MONTHS OLD ON VENUS!

ON VENUS A DAY IS LONGER THAN EIGHT EARTH MONTHS.

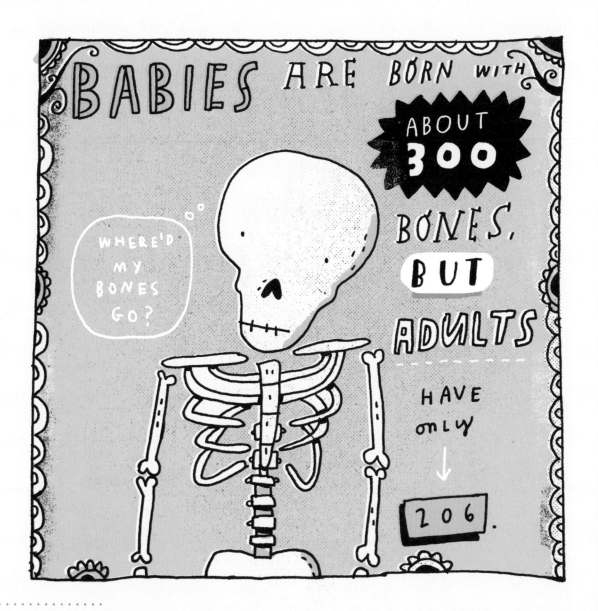

FACTS ABOUT: THE BODY

THE ACID IN YOUR STOMACH CAN DISSOLVE RAZOR BLADES.

HELLO.

YOUR NOSE PRODUCES 20 to 24 FLUID OUNCES OF MUCUS EVERY DAY.

WHEN YOU ARE AFRAID, YOUR EARS SECRETE MORE EARWAX THAN USUAL.

A PERSON'S TONGUE PRINT IS AS UNIQUE AS THEIR FINGERPRINT.

THE PRESSURE

IN YOUR HEART COULD SQUIRT BLOOD 30 FEET.

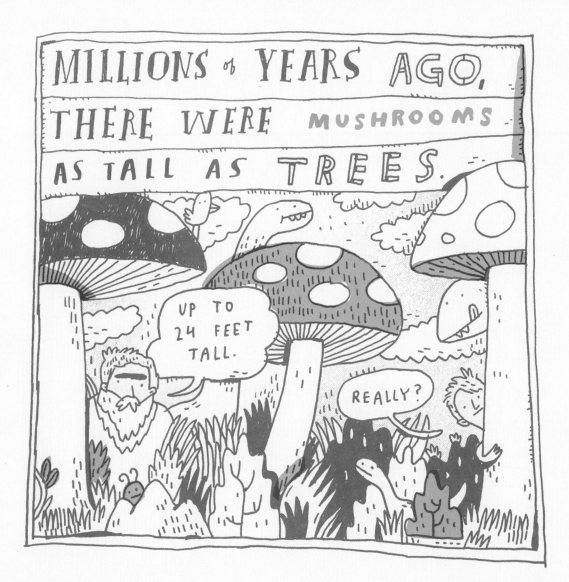

DURING ONE BATTLE of the CIVIL WAR, SOME of the SOLDIERS NOTICED their WOUNDS WERE **GLOWING.**

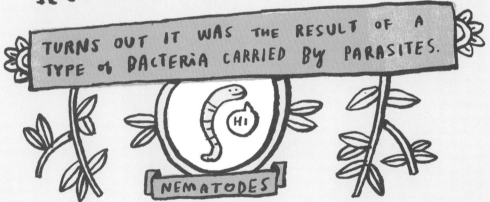

TURNS OUT IT WAS THE RESULT OF A TYPE of BACTERIA CARRIED BY PARASITES.

NEMATODES

A FEW things ABOUT BONES

1 OVER **90%** OF ANIMALS DON'T HAVE BACKBONES.

2 TOOTH ENAMEL IS **HARDER** than BONE.

3 the FUNNY BONE *IS ACTUALLY* A NERVE.

4 THE FIRST PROSTHETIC BONE WAS DEVELOPED in EGYPT 3,000 YEARS AGO: A BIG TOE.

THERE ARE **10** HUMAN BODY **PARTS** WITH ONLY **3** LETTERS.

EYE
EAR
JAW
LIP
GUM
RIB
ARM
HIP
LEG
TOE

DESERTS make up MORE THAN 20% of the EARTH'S SURFACE.

PART

FIVE

RANDOM FACTS ABOUT EVERYDAY THINGS:

WEIRD LAWS, TRADITIONS, and ORIGIN STORIES

BEFORE RUBBER ERASERS, PEOPLE USED BALLED-UP BREAD.

ONCE CALLED "WAIST OVERALLS"

JEANS

② 215 PAIRS CAN BE MADE FROM ONE BALE OF COTTON.

③ IN THE LATE 1800s MEN WOULD STORE TOBACCO in THEIR CUFFS.

① IN 1951 BING CROSBY WAS TURNED AWAY FROM A CANADIAN HOTEL FOR WEARING JEANS.

④ GEORGE W. BUSH BANNED JEANS IN THE OVAL OFFICE.

SOME THINGS ABOUT KNITTING

1 IT USED TO BE A MALE-ONLY OCCUPATION.

2 EARLY KNITTING NEEDLES WERE MADE of

GULP!

IVORY

BONE

OR TORTOISE SHELL.

3 IN 2005, A GROUP PLACED A 200-FOOT-LONG GIANT KNIT RABBIT IN the ITALIAN ALPS.

4 KNITTING WAS USED AS A FORM of CODE DURING WWI.

① SOME FOLKS USE **NIGHTINGALE** POOP to BRIGHTEN SKIN and **REMOVE** makeup.

② **FISH SCALES** ARE ADDED to SOME LIPSTICKS TO GIVE A "SHIMMER EFFECT."

③ **CLEOPATRA** WOULD SOAK the SAILS of HER SHIPS in **PERFUME.**

HATS

THE DUNCE CAP WAS DESIGNED to FUNNEL thoughts OR WISDOM into the "DUNCE."

DUNCE LY

VIKINGS NEVER WORE HORNED HELMETS.

SCRAMBLED ... OVER EASY ... UMM

THE 100 PLEATS ON A CHEF'S HAT ARE SAID TO REPRESENT the NUMBER OF WAYS they KNOW HOW to PREPARE an EGG.

4"
12"

IN the 18TH CENTURY MEN WORE TINY HATS ON TOP of THEIR WIGS.

WEIRD ONLINE AUCTIONS

1 A "HAUNTED" RUBBER DUCK — SOLD FOR $107

2 THE MEANING of LIFE — SOLD FOR $3

3 A SUIT of ARMOR FOR A GUINEA PIG

SOLD! $1,150

HEY LOOK! KITES

① IN THE 17TH AND 18TH CENTURIES, JAPAN HAD TO IMPOSE RESTRICTIONS ON KITES

BECAUSE PEOPLE PREFERRED KITE FLYING to WORKing.

② IN LATE 19TH- AND EARLY 20TH-CENTURY EUROPE, KITES WERE USED FOR MILITARY AERIAL OBSERVATION.

③ LARGEST KITE EVER FLOWN: TEN THOUSAND SQUARE FEET!

IT'S AGAINST *the* LAW *to* FALL ASLEEP *in* A CHEESE FACTORY *in* ILLINOIS.

MORE TOTALLY WEIRD LAWS

IN DELAWARE, IT'S ILLEGAL TO SELL THE FUR OF A DOMESTIC DOG OR CAT.

IN KENTUCKY, EVERY LEGISLATOR, PUBLIC OFFICER, AND LAWYER MUST TAKE AN OATH STATING THAT THEY HAVE NOT FOUGHT IN A DUEL WITH DEADLY WEAPONS.

DOES THAT MEAN IT'S LEGAL IN OTHER PLACES?!

EWWW

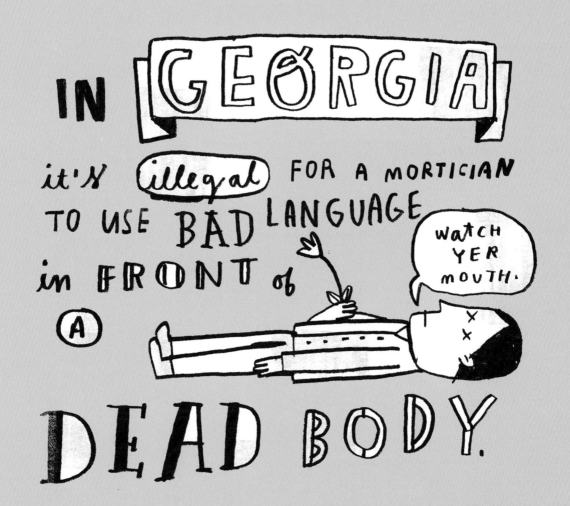

IN 1914, A FIVE-YEAR-OLD GIRL WAS (MAILED) TO HER GRANDPARENTS

WHEN HER PARENTS REALIZED that PARCEL POST WAS CHEAPER than A TRAIN TICKET (JUST 53 CENTS!).

MAIL CALL!

ELVIS STAMPS ARE the BEST SELLING COMMEMORATIVE STAMPS.

LIVE SCORPIONS CAN BE SENT THROUGH the MAIL, BUT SPIDERS CAN'T BE.

AW, MAN.

FIRST ENVELOPES? IN 2000 BC, BABYLONIANS PROTECTED IMPORTANT DOCUMENTS WITH CLAY WRAPPERS.

MAIL IN THE GRAND CANYON IS DELIVERED BY MULE.

IT RAINS FISH
ONCE A YEAR in
YORO, HONDURAS.*

* ALTHOUGH IT'S LIKELY THAT HEAVY RAINSTORMS AND FLOODING ARE BRINGING THE FISH INTO THE STREET, SOME LOCALS BELIEVE IT'S A MIRACLE.

MOMS

① AN ELEPHANT MOTHER'S PREGNANCY CAN LAST UP TO 22 MONTHS!

② the OLDEST WOMAN to BECOME a MOTHER WAS IN HER SEVENTIES!

③ IN SERBIA CHILDREN TIE UP their MOM ON MOTHER'S DAY, and they RELEASE HER ONLY if SHE GIVES them TREATS.

IN THE NURSERY RHYME, HUMPTY DUMPTY IS NEVER CALLED an EGG.

then WHAT AM I?

SOME HISTORIANS BELIEVE it's ACTUALLY ABOUT A CANNON USED DURING the ENGLISH CIVIL WAR of 1642-1651.

YUMMY

BLOOD

HAS BEEN USED AS AN EGG SUBSTITUTE in BAKING

and in **MAKING ICE CREAM.**

THE OLDEST KNOWN GLOBE THAT INCLUDES THE NEW WORLD IS ENGRAVED ON TWO CONJOINED HALVES of **OSTRICH EGGS.**

OOPS.

A HEN WILL TURN HER EGG **50** TIMES A DAY SO THE YOLK DOESN'T STICK TO THE SIDE.

ORIGINALLY, CARS WERE SEEN as THE "GREEN" SOLUTION, BECAUSE HORSES WERE CAUSING TOO MUCH POLLUTION . . .

WITH THEIR **POOP.**

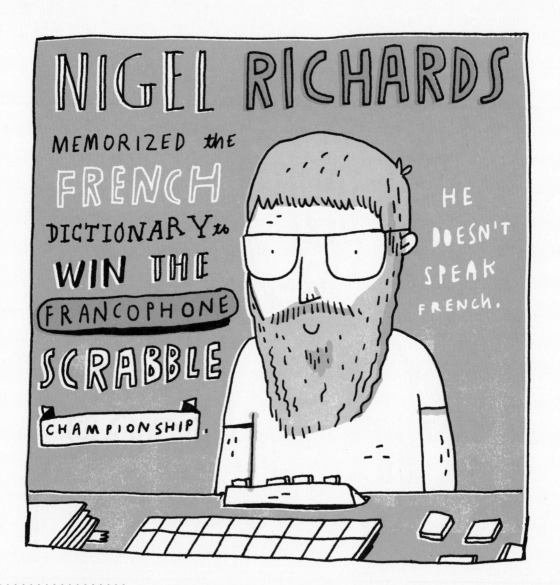

①  THE NAME **JENGA** COMES FROM A SWAHILI WORD MEANING "TO BUILD."

②  THE RECORD FOR THE LONGEST MARATHON PLAYING A BOARD GAME IS **61** HOURS + **2** MINUTES OF STRAT-O-MATIC BASEBALL.

③

YAHTZEE WAS CREATED BY A RICH COUPLE WHO MADE UP the GAME While ON their **YACHT.**

OH, ALSO: THERE IS A MONOPOLY SET MADE OUT OF:

- 23 KARAT GOLD
- RUBIES • SAPPHIRES
- DIAMONDS → WORTH 2 MILLION BUCKS!

BAGPIPES

TRADITIONALLY, they WERE MADE FROM the WHOLE SKIN of an ANIMAL.

♪

THEY'RE LOUDER THAN A JACKHAMMER

IN BULGARIA, IT'S CALLED A GAIDA.

THEY'VE BEEN AROUND SINCE 100 BC.

AC/DC'S LEAD SINGER USED TO PLAY BAGPIPES AT THEIR SHOWS, UNTIL A CROWD DESTROYED HIS INSTRUMENT.

THE BANJO

ORIGINATED in WEST AFRICA.

THE SONG "DUELING BANJOS" in THE MOVIE DELIVERANCE FEATURES A

GUITAR AND A BANJO

⟶

NOT 2 BANJOS.

THE FIRST BANJO INSTRUCTION BOOK WAS PUBLISHED in 1848.

JOHN LENNON'S FIRST INSTRUMENT

ALSO KNOWN AS:

THE BANZA

IN HAITI.

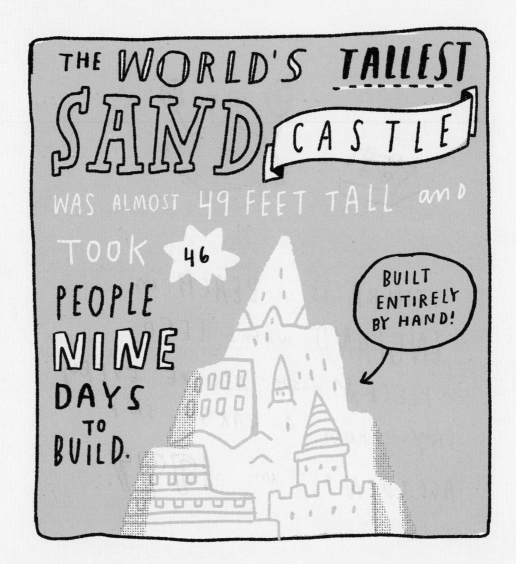

THERE IS A BEACH in ENGLAND WHERE LEGO PIECES WASH ASHORE EVERY DAY FROM A CARGO ship ACCIDENT in 1997.

"HELLO" WAS A WORD USED to EXPRESS SURPRISE BEFORE THOMAS EDISON SUGGESTED USING it TO START a TELEPHONE CALL.

HELLO! WHAT'S THIS NOW?

ALEXANDER GRAHAM BELL WANTED FOLKS TO USE "AHOY."

SIGH

EDISON

BELL

TELEPHONE TIDBITS

1 THE first MOBILE PHONE COST $4,000.

2 MODERN CELL PHONES ARE MORE POWERFUL than THE COMPUTERS USED To LAND APOLLO 11 ON the MOON.

3 IN 2011, A BOY in NORWAY ESCAPED WOLVES BY PLAYING A CREED SONG ON HIS CELL PHONE.

I COULDN'T TAKE iT!

IN 2012, TWO BOYS FOUND A BONE FROM A 13,000-YEAR-OLD **MASTODON** WHILE FISHING in MICHIGAN.

WHEN GET-TOGETHERS in SCHOOL GYMs BECAME POPULAR in the LATE 1950s, DANCERS WERE REQUIRED to REMOVE their SHOES to PROTECT the WOODEN FLOORS. THUS THE NICKNAME: SOCK HOP.

IN ANCIENT GREECE, SOCKS WERE MADE OUT OF MATTED ANIMAL FUR.

PANTYHOSE WERE ORIGINALLY CALLED PANTI-LEGS.

ALBERT EINSTEIN HATED WEARING SOCKS.

IF YOU RUB YOUR FEET WITH GARLIC, YOU WILL TASTE IT.

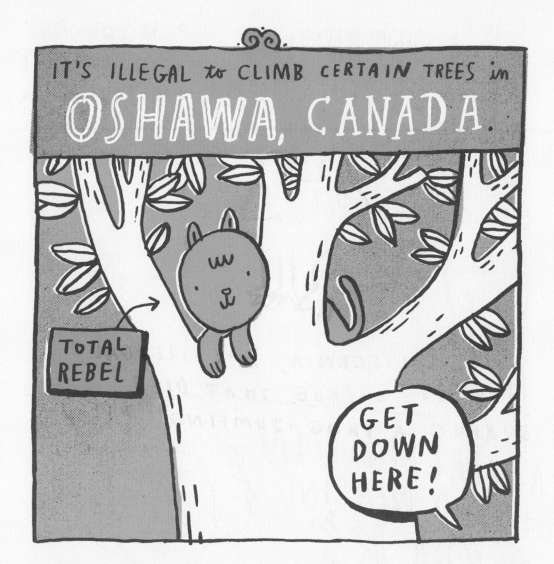

IN CALIFORNIA, it's ILLEGAL
TO EAT A FROG THAT DIES
DURING A FROG-JUMPING CONTEST.

WEIRD MUSEUMS

THAT ACTUALLY EXIST!

the BRITISH
LAWNMOWER
M U S E U M
(ENGLAND)

NATIONAL
MUSTARD
MUSEUM
(WISCONSIN, USA)

THE MUSEUM of
BROKEN
RELATIONSHIPS

ORIGINALLY STARTED
in CROATIA (AND
NOW WITH A BRANCH in
LOS ANGELES), this
MUSEUM SHOW-
CASES OBJECTS
FROM BAD
BREAKUPS.

SULABH iNternational
MUSEUM OF TOILETS
(INDIA)

LE MUSÉE DES
VAMPIRES
F R A N C E

:H

TWINE BALL MUSEUM
(MINNESOTA, USA)

A FEW WORDS OF

APPRECIATION

THANK YOU to the FOLKS WHO GAVE me ALMOST DAILY FEEDBACK ON this PROJECT FOR MORE than A YEAR --> CALEB MORRIS, JOSHUA HATHAWAY, JOSH BRANHAM + BRANDON FORBES.

HUGE thanks to MY AWESOME EDITOR SAM AND to DANIEL and the OTHER FOLKS at WORKMAN.

OH, AND ALSO, THESE TWO LADIES ARE THE BEST!

KATRIN

ALLISTER

ADDITIONAL RESEARCH DONE BY COLLEEN FINN! • HELP WITH JAPANESE CHARACTERS BY NICK AKERS.

SOME OF THE STUFF I USED to MAKE this BOOK:

HAND·BOOK SKETCHBOOKS

RAPIDOGRAPH PEN + INK

MECHANICAL PENCILS

PENTEL SIGN PEN

INK MIXED WITH WATER IN AN ARTICHOKE HEARTS JAR

PHOTOSHOP

FACTS

IPAD

FACTS

W/ASTROPAD APP

ABOUT THE
AUTHOR

MIKE LOWERY

HAS ILLUSTRATED DOZENS of BOOKS FOR READERS OF ALL AGES and IS THE CREATOR OF the DOODLE ADVENTURES® SERIES. HE IS A FOUNDING MEMBER of PAPER GHOST, AN ILLUSTRATION-FOCUSED GALLERY IN ATLANTA, GA, WHERE HE LIVES WITH HIS WIFE AND DAUGHTER.